W9-BGJ-691

PRO SPORTS
BIOGRAPHIES

J
B
JAM

# LEBRON JAMES

by Elizabeth Raum

AMICUS HIGH INTEREST • AMICUS INK

Amicus High Interest and Amicus Ink are imprints of Amicus
P.O. Box 1329, Mankato, MN 56002
www.amicuspublishing.us

Library of Congress Cataloging-in-Publication Data
Names: Raum, Elizabeth, author.
Title: Lebron James / by Elizabeth Raum.
Description: Mankato, Minnesota : Amicus, 2018. | Series: Amicus High
 Interest. Pro Sports Biographies | Includes index. | Audience: K to Grade 3.
Identifiers: LCCN 2016058345 (print) | LCCN 2017000381 (ebook) | ISBN
 9781681511382 (library binding) | ISBN 9781681521695 (pbk.) | ISBN
 9781681512280 (ebook)
Subjects: LCSH: James, LeBron--Juvenile literature. | African American
 basketball players--Biography--Juvenile literature. | Basketball players--
 United States--Biography--Juvenile literature.
Classification: LCC GV884.J36 R38 2018 (print) | LCC GV884.J36 (ebook) |
 DDC 796.323092 [B] --dc23
LC record available at https://lccn.loc.gov/2016058345

Photo Credits: Jason Miller/Contributor/Getty Images Sport cover;
Ezra Shaw/Getty Images 2, 4; AP Photo/Bruce Schwartzman 7; David
Saffran/Sports Chrome/Newscom 8–9; AP Photo/Tony Dejak 10–11;
        Gary Coronado/ZUMAPRESS/Newscom 12; Gouhier–
        Guibbaud–JMP/ABACA/Newscom 15, 22; AP Photo/
        Alex Menendez 16–17; AP Photo/Eric Risberg 19;
        Marcio Sanchez/Associated Press/POOL/EPA/
        Newscom 20–21

        Editor: Wendy Dieker
        Designer: Aubrey Harper
        Photo Researcher: Holly Young

        Printed in the United States
        of America

HC 10 9 8 7 6 5 4 3 2 1
PB 10 9 8 7 6 5 4 3 2 1

# TABLE OF CONTENTS

MVP                           5

Playing Ball                  6

Chosen One                    9

Pro Ball                      10

Winning in Miami              13

Team USA                      14

Helping Out                   17

Family Man                    18

Ohio Love                     21

Just the Facts                22

Words to Know                 23

Learn More                    24

Index                         24

# MVP

The Cleveland Cavaliers won the 2016 **NBA** Finals. Who led the team? LeBron James. In game seven, he scored 27 points. He grabbed 11 **rebounds** and made 11 **assists**. No wonder he was the **MVP**.

The Cavaliers are called the Cavs for short.

# PLAYING BALL

LeBron James was born in Akron, Ohio, in 1984. He joined a basketball team in fourth grade. He loved it. He went to St. Vincent–St. Mary High School to play basketball. He helped the team win state titles.

# CHOSEN ONE

James was an amazing high school player. *Sports Illustrated* magazine called him "The Chosen One." They knew he'd be famous. Pro **scouts** started coming to his games. NBA players even came to watch!

# PRO BALL

James joined the pros right out of high school. He was the number one **draft pick** in 2003. The Cavs, an Ohio team, chose him.

James was the first Cavs player to win the NBA Rookie of the Year Award.

# WINNING IN MIAMI

James played for the Cavs until 2010. Then, he moved to Miami. He played for the Heat. He led them to two NBA titles. In 2014, he returned home to Ohio to play for the Cavs.

# TEAM USA

James also played in the Olympics three times. He helped Team USA win the bronze medal in 2004. In 2008 and 2012, they won gold.

James was only 19 when he played in his first Olympics in 2004.

# HELPING OUT

James grew up with only one parent. But adults in his life helped him be great. He wants to be someone who helps kids, too. He raises money to help fix gyms. He tells kids to stay in school.

# FAMILY MAN

James has a wife and kids. He has two sons and a daughter. James tells his kids to dream big. He works hard to be the dad he never had. They know he cares.

19

# OHIO LOVE

In 2016, James led the Cavs to victory. It was the first time the team won the NBA Finals. Fans want LeBron James to stay. He plans to do just that. "I love it here," he says.

# JUST THE FACTS

**Born:** December 30, 1984

**Hometown:** Akron, Ohio

**Joined the Pros:** 2003

**Position:** Forward

**Stats:** www.nba.com/players/lebron/james/2544

**Accomplishments:**

- NBA Rookie of the Year: 2004

- NBA Scoring Champion: 2008

- NBA All Star appearances: 13, voted MVP 2006, 2008

- NBA Most Valuable Player: 2009, 2010, 2012, 2013

- NBA Finals wins: 2012, 2013, 2016, voted MVP all three years

- Olympic medalist: 2004 (bronze), 2008 (gold), 2012 (gold)

# WORDS TO KNOW

**assists** – in basketball, a move that helps another player make a basket

**draft pick** – a high school or college athlete chosen to join an NBA team

**MVP** – short for Most Valuable Player; an award given to the player who helped the team the most.

**NBA** – short for National Basketball Association, the organization that makes rules for professional basketball in the United States

**rebounds** – in basketball, when a player grabs the ball after someone missed a basket

**scout** – a person who watches amateur athletes and makes lists of athletes who would be good pro players

# LEARN MORE

## Books
Frisch, Nate. *The Story of the Cleveland Cavaliers*. Mankato, Minn.: Creative Education, 2015.

Gregory, Josh. *LeBron James*. New York: Bearport, 2014.

Maurer, Tracy. *LeBron James*. North Mankato, Minn.: Capstone, 2016.

## Websites
**LeBron James Family Foundation**
http://lebronjamesfamilyfoundation.org

**LeBron James Official Website**
www.lebronjames.com

# INDEX

awards 5, 10, 14

Cleveland Cavaliers 5, 10, 13, 21

family 17, 18

going pro 10

high school 6, 9

LeBron James Family Foundation 17

Miami Heat 13

NBA 5, 9, 10, 13, 21

Olympics 14